★ ★ ★ ★ ★ **MILITARY FAMILIES** ★ ★ ★ ★ ★

My Dad Is in the
ARMY

PETER KOHL

PowerKiDS
press™

New York

Published in 2016 by The Rosen Publishing Group, Inc.
29 East 21st Street, New York, NY 10010

First Edition

Editor: Sarah Machajewski
Book Design: Katelyn Heinle

Photo Credits: Cover, pp. 5 (soldier), 22 Jupiterimages/Thinkstock.com; cover backdrop, p. 1 David Smart/Shutterstock.com; pp. 3–4, 6, 8, 10, 12, 14, 16, 18, 20, 22, 24 (camouflage texture) Casper1774/Shutterstock.com; p. 7 (top) Stocktrek Images/ Getty Images; pp. 7 (bottom), 13 (both), 15 (top) courtesy of U.S. Army Flickr; p. 9 (top) Goodluz/Shutterstock.com; p. 9 (bottom) Oleg Zabielin/Shutterstock.com; p. 11 Chris Hondros/Getty Images News/Getty Images; p. 15 (bottom) kanin.studio/ Shutterstock.com; p. 17 Mark Edward Atkinson/Blend Images/Getty Images; p. 19 (top) Siobhan Connally/Moment/Getty Images; p. 19 (bottom) SHAH MARAI/ AFP/Getty Images; p. 21 Monkey Business Images/Shutterstock.com.

Cataloging-in-Publication Data

Kohl, Peter.
My dad is in the Army / by Peter Kohl.
p. cm. — (Military families)
Includes index.
ISBN 978-1-5081-4434-2 (pbk.)
ISBN 978-1-5081-4435-9 (6-pack)
ISBN 978-1-5081-4436-6 (library binding)
1. United States. Army — Juvenile literature. 2. Soldiers — United States — Juvenile literature. 3. Children of military personnel — United States — Juvenile literature. I. Kohl, Peter. II. Title.
UA25.K64 2016
355.00973—d23

DIRECT

MAR 0 9 2016

Manufactured in the United States of America

CPSIA Compliance Information: Batch #BW16PK: For Further Information contact Rosen Publishing, New York, New York at 1-800-237-9932

CONTENTS

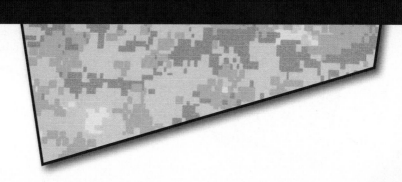

MY DAD, THE HERO

The United States military has five branches. Thousands of men and women serve in each branch. My dad serves in the United States Army. He's **dedicated** his life to **protecting** our country. My dad is one of the bravest people I know.

My dad joined the army before I was born. He has **defended** our country all over the world and at home, too. It's not always easy having a dad in the army, but I know his job is important. A lot of people have jobs just like my dad's. Let's find out more about them.

MY DAD IS SOMETIMES GONE FOR WEEKS AT A TIME. IT'S NICE WHEN HE COMES HOME!

THE ARMED FORCES

The U.S. military is sometimes called the "armed forces." These forces are the five branches of the military. The army is one branch. The others are the navy, coast guard, air force, and Marine **Corps**. The armed forces work together to protect the United States and its people.

The army is the largest military branch. It's the U.S. military's land-based force, which means soldiers like my dad fight missions on land using **weapons** and machines such as tanks. The army defends the United States if it's attacked or **invaded**. It's often called to fight in other countries, too.

★★★
MILITARY MATTERS
The air force fights in the air. The navy and coast guard fight at sea. The Marine Corps fights in the air, on land, and at sea.

THE U.S. ARMY IS READY TO DEFEND OUR COUNTRY IN TIMES OF **CRISIS**, BOTH AT HOME AND OVERSEAS.

A Long History

Along with being the largest military branch, the army is also the oldest. It traces its roots back to the Continental army, which fought for the 13 colonies during the American Revolution. Congress voted to replace the Continental army with the United States Army on June 3, 1784.

Today, the army is split into three groups—the army, the Army Reserve, and the Army National Guard. The army has **active-duty** soldiers who work for the army full time. The reserve and National Guard have citizens who work for the army part time, but also have regular jobs.

★★★
Military Matters
Though the army was officially founded in 1784, many people say it's been around since 1775—before the United States was even a country!

ARMY RESERVE
SOLDIER

ACTIVE-DUTY
SOLDIER

ACTIVE-DUTY SOLDIERS, RESERVE SOLDIERS, AND NATIONAL GUARD SOLDIERS WORK TOGETHER TO SUPPORT ONE OF THE WORLD'S LARGEST AND MOST POWERFUL ARMIES.

How to Join

   As of 2014, the U.S. Army had about 675,000 **enlisted** soldiers between the regular army and the reserve. Soldiers have to meet certain requirements to join. To join the army, you must be between 18 and 35 years old, but you can join at 17 with permission from your parents.

   Generally, soldiers must be U.S. citizens. However, people who have lawfully come here from another country can enlist. Finally, soldiers have to have a high school diploma, which is something that shows you've completed a high school education. The army may also accept people with a GED, which is much like a high school diploma.

MY DAD SAID HE TALKED TO A RECRUITER BEFORE HE JOINED THE ARMY. AN ARMY RECRUITER WORKS WITH FUTURE SOLDIERS AND THEIR FAMILIES TO SEE IF JOINING THE ARMY IS RIGHT FOR THEM. RECRUITERS ANSWER IMPORTANT QUESTIONS FAMILIES MAY HAVE.

Army Training

When my dad joined the army, he had to go to Basic **Combat** Training (BCT) for 10 weeks. BCT is sometimes known as "boot camp." This is where soldiers learn the skills needed to serve in the army, such as how to fight and how to use weapons. They also learn problem-solving skills and how to work as part of a team.

After my dad graduated from boot camp, he went to Advanced Individual Training (AIT). Here, he trained for the job he has in the army. He's an intelligence officer, which means he gathers important knowledge about the forces the army fights.

★★★
Military Matters
In the army, men and women can train to become either enlisted soldiers or officers.

MY DAD JOINED THE ARMY BEFORE I WAS BORN, BUT MY MOM SAID IT WAS HARD WHEN HE WENT AWAY TO BASIC TRAINING. SHE MISSED HIM A LOT AND COULDN'T SEE HIM FOR 10 WEEKS! HE WAS HAPPY TO HAVE HER SUPPORT BACK HOME.

A Career with the Army

My dad is an intelligence officer, but that's just one of the careers a person can have. The army offers more than 150 careers. Soldiers can be **engineers**, computer specialists, military police, accountants, and more.

The army also has doctors and nurses. They work hard to keep soldiers healthy and help them when they're hurt. There are also chaplains, which is another word for priests. Every job plays a part in helping the army run smoothly. Many people join the army because of the job opportunities it offers. Skills learned through the army can later be used at a **civilian** job, too.

WHEN YOU THINK OF THE ARMY, YOU MAY THINK OF SOLDIERS FIGHTING IN COMBAT. THEY'RE CALLED INFANTRY SOLDIERS. TRAINING FOR THIS JOB IS A LITTLE BIT DIFFERENT THAN REGULAR TRAINING. BOOT CAMP AND AIT ARE COMBINED INTO ONE SCHOOL IN FORT BENNING, GEORGIA.

Life on an Army Base

Since my dad's full-time job is working for the army, it affects my whole family's life. It determines where we live and how often we get to see him.

We live in a house on an army base. An army base is where soldiers train and equipment is held. My neighborhood is full of kids whose moms and dads are in the army. We go to school in the town closest to the army base, and our base has its own library. It feels a lot like a regular neighborhood. The only difference is we live around a lot of military families.

IT'S NICE LIVING ON AN ARMY BASE, BECAUSE MY FRIENDS KNOW WHAT IT'S LIKE TO HAVE A PARENT IN THE ARMY. THEY KNOW WHAT I MEAN WHEN I SAY I'M PROUD OF MY DAD OR WHEN I SAY I MISS HIM.

All About Deployment

My dad is my hero because he's dedicated his life to serving and protecting our country. I'm really proud of him for being an army officer, but some parts of it are hard. One of the hardest parts is when he's deployed.

Deployment is when the army sends my dad on a mission away from home. Deployment can last just a few months, but sometimes it lasts more than a year. We don't get to talk to him much, and sometimes we worry if he's safe. A lot of military families think deployment is the hardest part of the job.

★★★
Military Matters
If your parent is deployed, it's okay to feel sad, mad, or lonely. Talking about it with your family or a trusted adult can help you feel better.

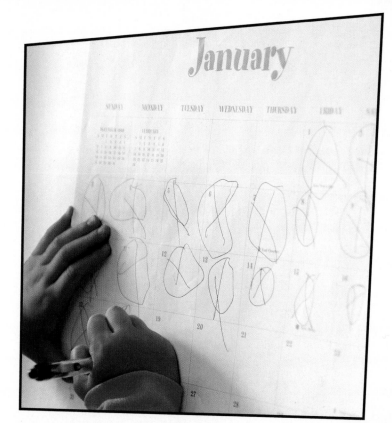

WHEN MY DAD IS DEPLOYED, MY MOM AND I SEND HIM CARE PACKAGES. WE WRITE HIM LETTERS AND SEND HIM PICTURES AND OTHER STUFF FROM HOME. WE ALSO KEEP A CALENDAR THAT SAYS WHEN MY DAD IS COMING BACK. I LOVE CROSSING OFF THE DAYS!

LIFE FOR ARMY FAMILIES

If you don't have a parent in the military, you may wonder what it's like. We're just like any other family, except my dad has to go away sometimes. When he comes back from being deployed, we do normal things such as eat dinner together, watch movies, and hang out. It makes me really happy when my dad comes home.

Moving is a big part of being in an army family. Sometimes my dad's job sends him to different states, and we have to go with him. It's hard leaving behind my friends, but I know my dad's job is really important.

ARMY FAMILIES ARE USED TO MOVING TO DIFFERENT PLACES. IT CAN BE SAD, BUT IT CAN BE FUN, TOO. IT'S A GREAT WAY TO MEET NEW PEOPLE AND SEE DIFFERENT PARTS OF OUR COUNTRY.

Supporting My Dad

Army soldiers and officers usually serve between two and six years, but they can reenlist if they want to stay in the army longer. My dad plans to stay with the army for as long as he can. He feels it's his job to serve and protect our country, and my family supports him.

Servicemen and servicewomen in every military branch make a lot of **sacrifices** for our country. Their families make sacrifices, too. It's not always easy, but we understand why it's important. I'm proud of my dad for serving in the U.S. Army. He will always be my hero!

GLOSSARY

active duty: Having to do with full-time service in the military. Also, full-time service in the military.

civilian: Having to do with a person not in the armed services or police force.

combat: Fighting between armed forces.

corps: A group within a branch of a military organization that does a particular kind of work.

crisis: A time of difficulty, trouble, or danger.

dedicate: To give yourself to a certain task or purpose.

defend: To keep safe from harm or danger.

engineer: A person who creates, builds, or works on engines, machines, and public works.

enlist: To join.

invade: To enter a country in order to occupy it or take it over.

protect: To keep safe.

sacrifice: Something given up for a larger purpose.

weapon: Something used to cause harm.

INDEX

WEBSITES

Due to the changing nature of Internet links, PowerKids Press has developed an online list of websites related to the subject of this book. This site is updated regularly. Please use this link to access the list: www.powerkidslinks.com/mili/dada